BIG-NOTE PIANO

Shout Praises Kids Songbook

Page	Title
2	All About You
7	Everyday
19	Friend Of God
12	God Is Great
24	I Will Boast
29	Majestic
37	Mighty To Save
32	My Best Friend
42	Shout To The Lord
46	This God He Is Our God
52	Trust In The Lord
56	We Lift You Up
60	Worship You Forever
63	You Are Good
68	Your Name

ISBN 978-1-4234-3992-9

HAL•LEONARD® CORPORATION
7777 W. BLUEMOUND RD. P.O. BOX 13819 MILWAUKEE, WI 53213

For all works contained herein:
Unauthorized copying, arranging, adapting, recording or public performance is an infringement of copyright. Infringers are liable under the law.

Visit Hal Leonard Online at
www.halleonard.com

ALL ABOUT YOU

Words and Music by ISRAEL HOUGHTON
and CINDY CRUSE-RATCLIFF

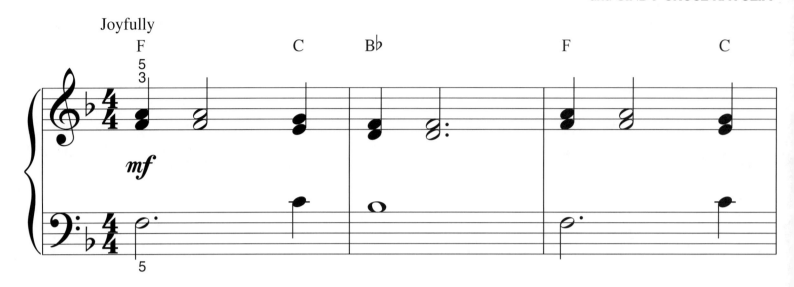
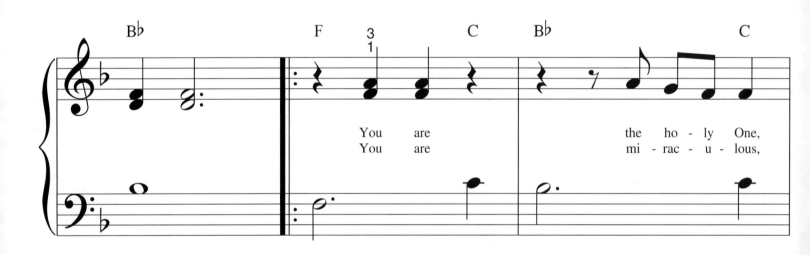
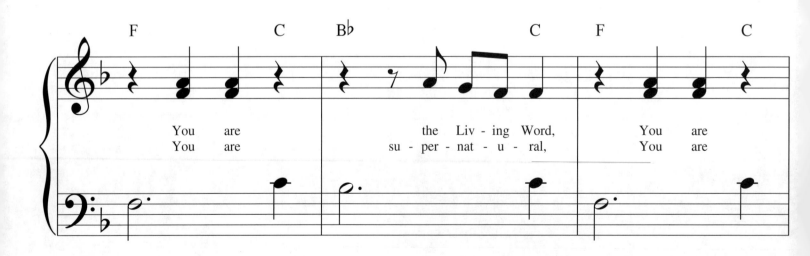

© 2001 My Other Publishing Company/BMI, Lakewood Ministries Music/BMI (both admin. by Integrity's Praise! Music) and Integrity's Praise! Music/BMI
c/o Integrity Media, Inc., 1000 Cody Road, Mobile, AL 36695
All Rights Reserved   International Copyright Secured   Used by Permission

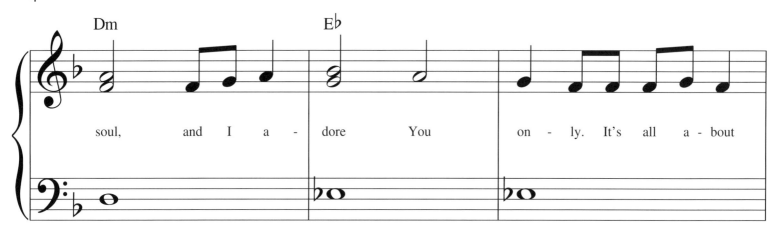
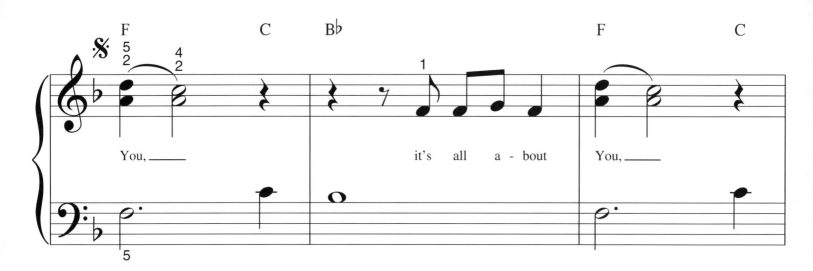
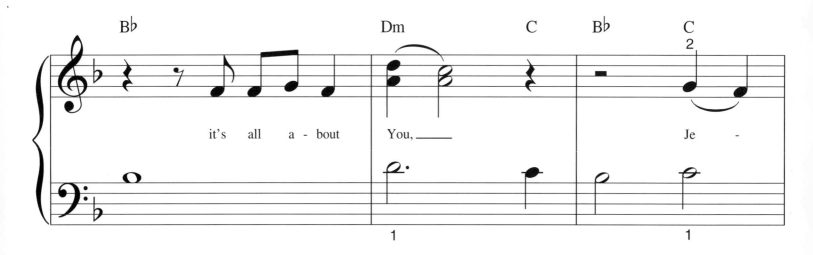
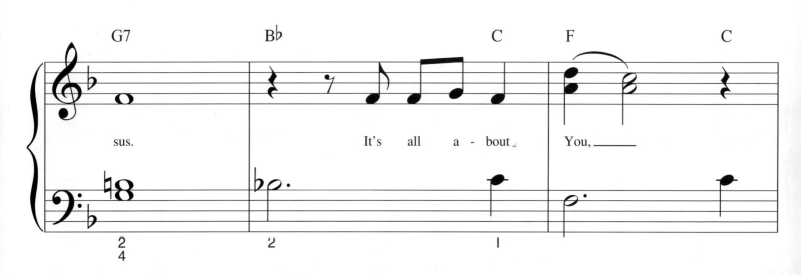

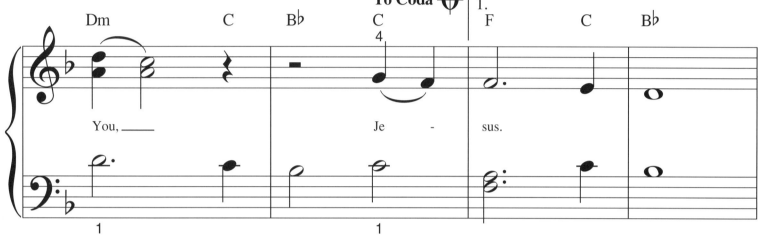
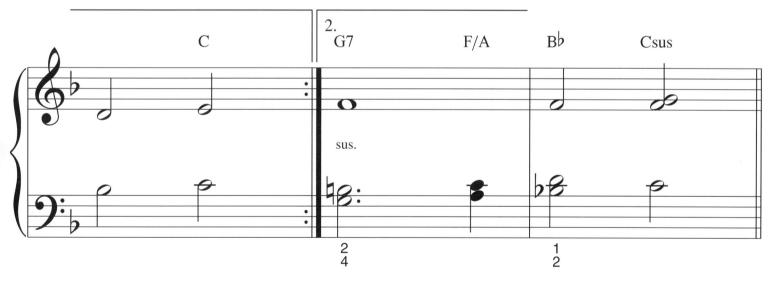
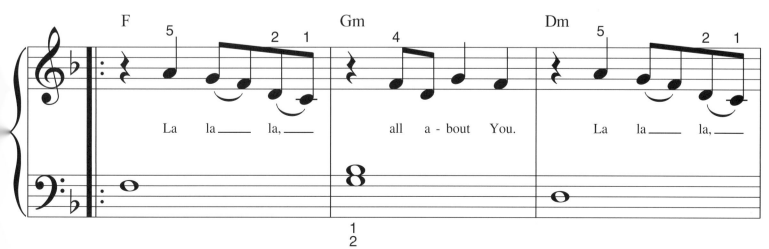

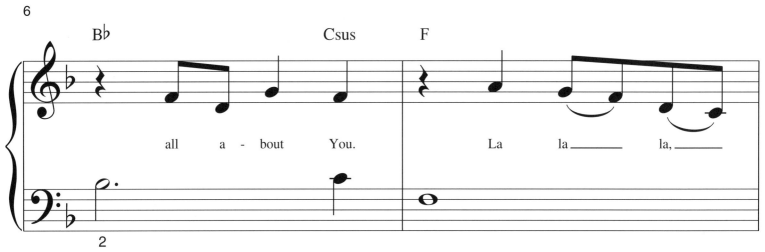
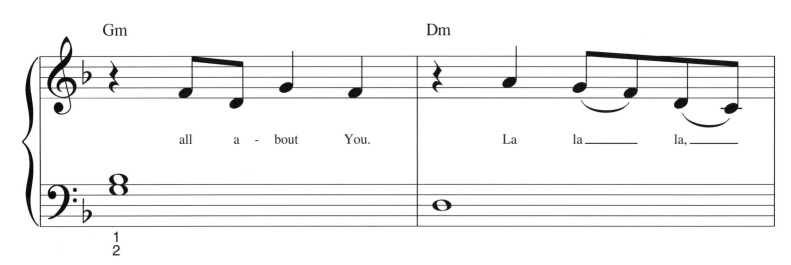
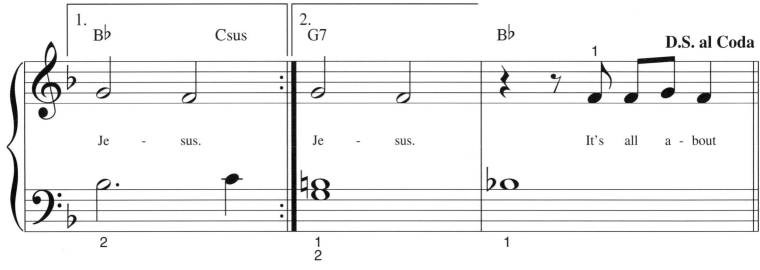
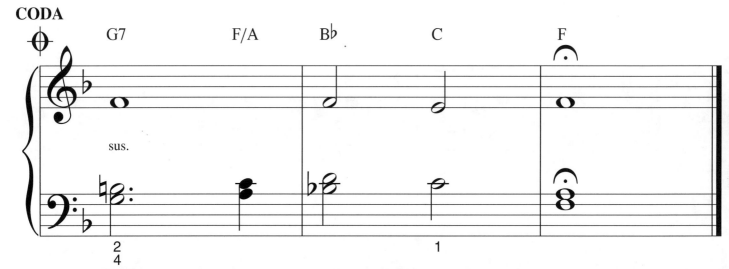

EVERYDAY

Words and Music by
JOEL HOUSTON

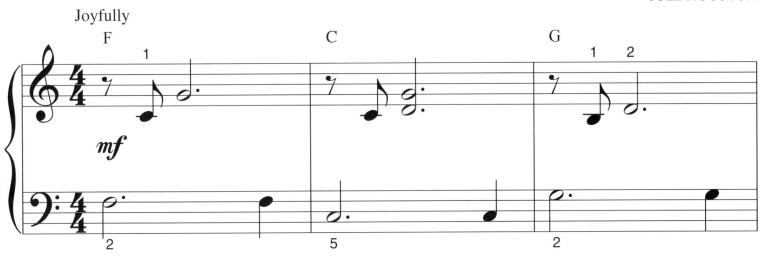

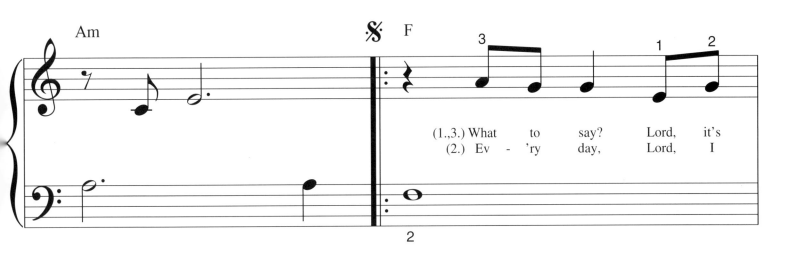

(1.,3.) What to say? Lord, it's
(2.) Ev-'ry day, Lord, I

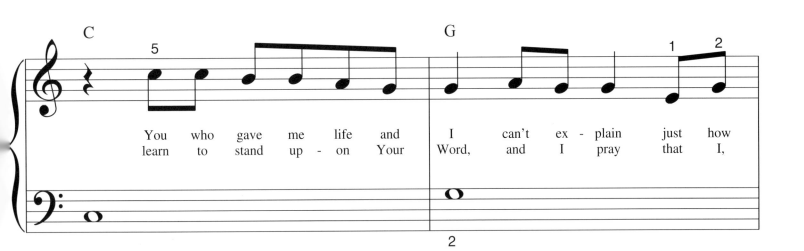

You who gave me life and I can't ex-plain just how
learn to stand up-on Your Word, and I pray that I,

© 1999 Joel Houston and Hillsong Publishing (admin. in the United States and Canada by Integrity's Hosanna! Music)/ASCAP
c/o Integrity Media, Inc., 1000 Cody Road, Mobile, AL 36695
All Rights Reserved   International Copyright Secured   Used by Permission

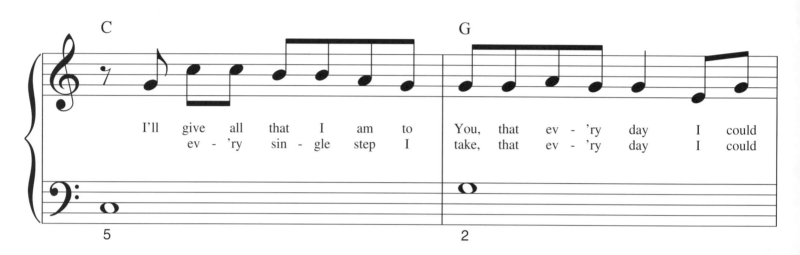
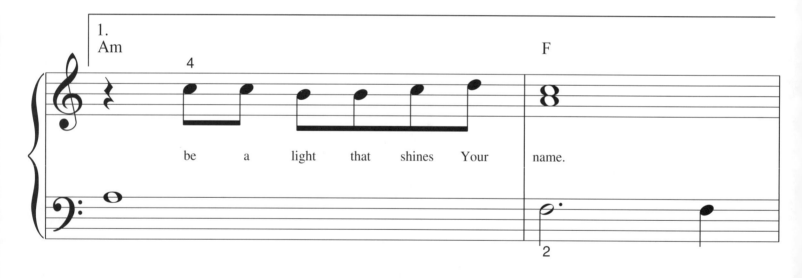

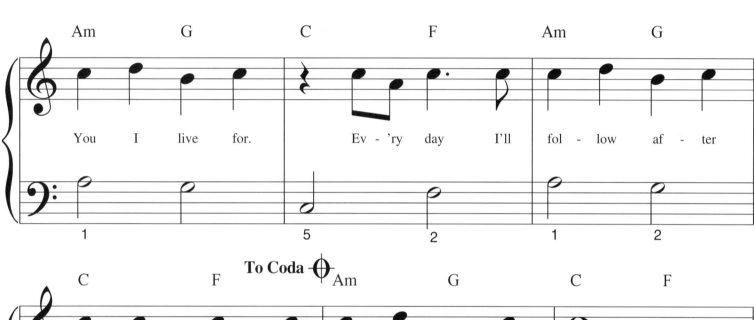

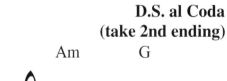

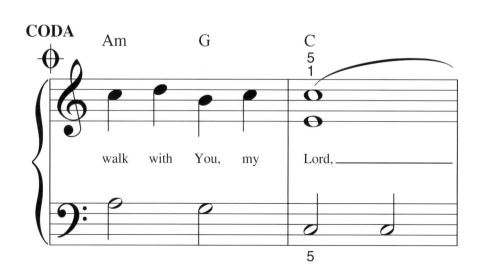

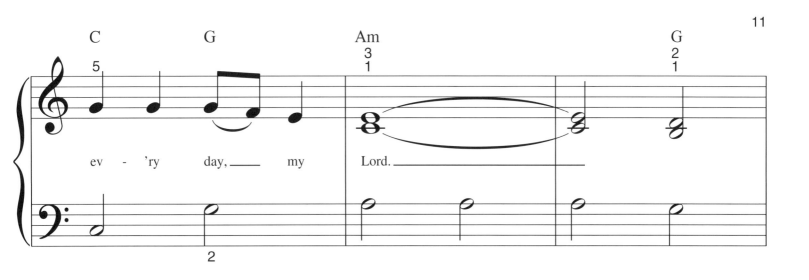

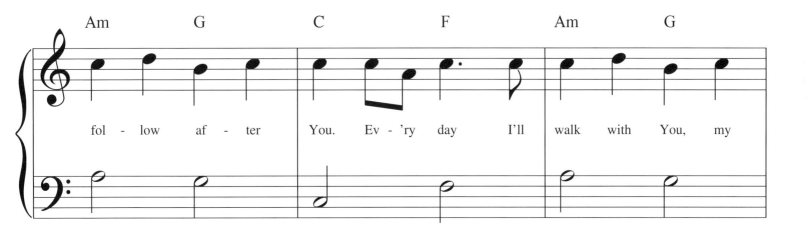
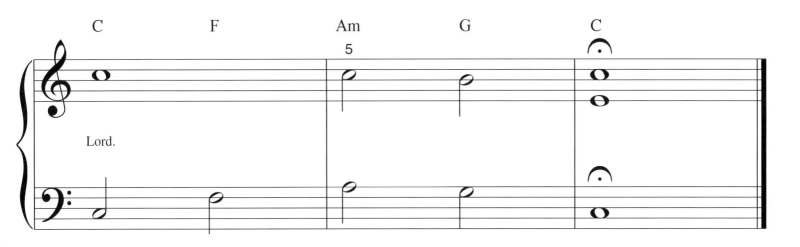

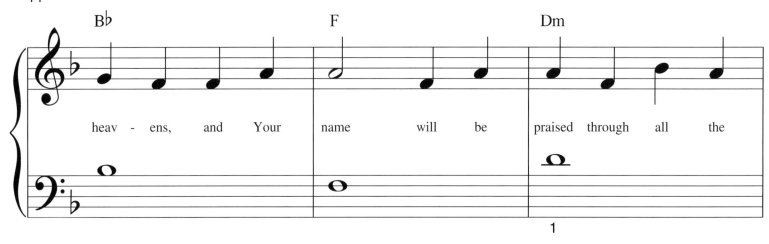
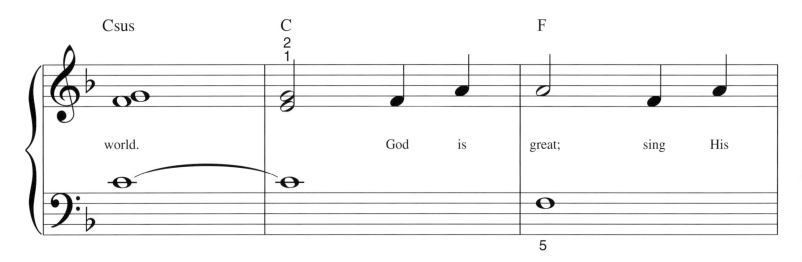
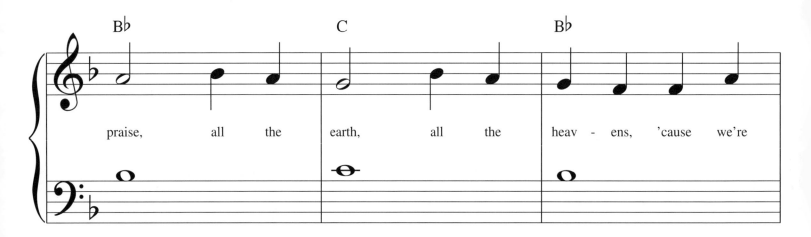
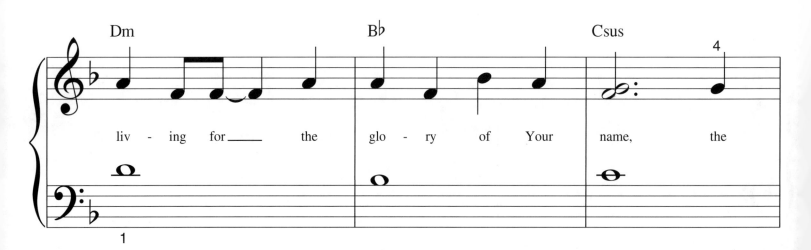

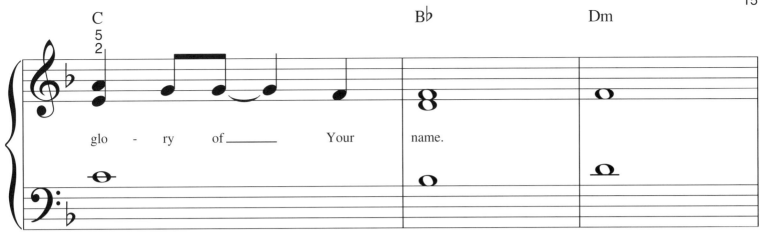
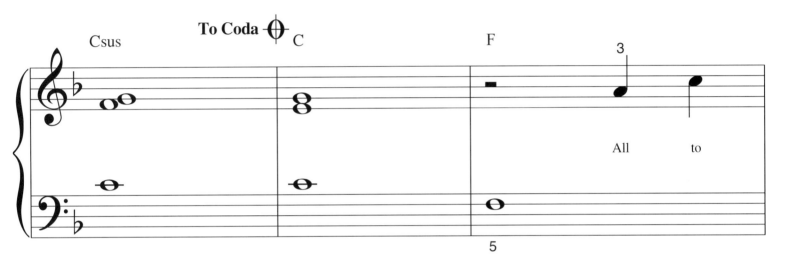
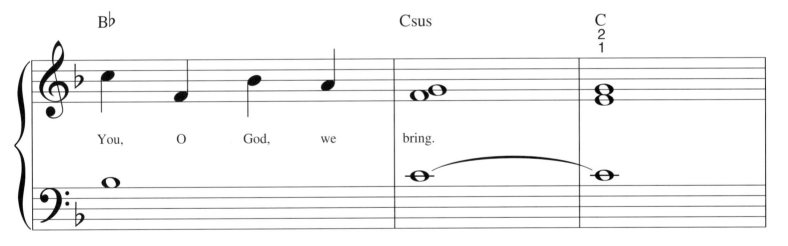
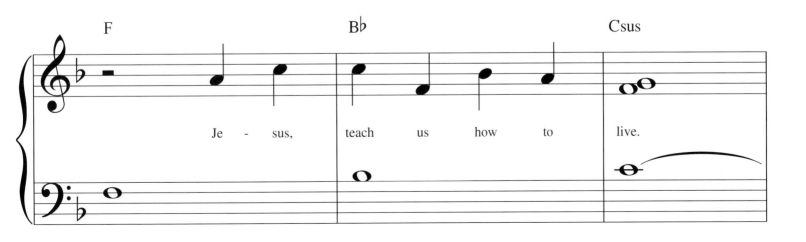

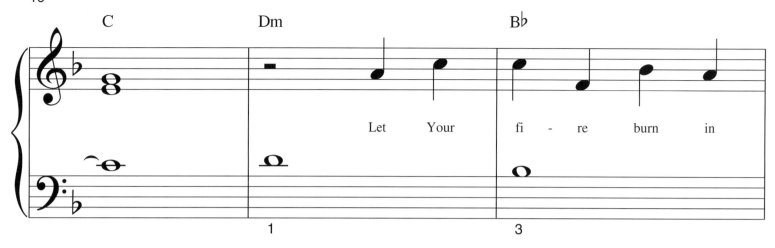
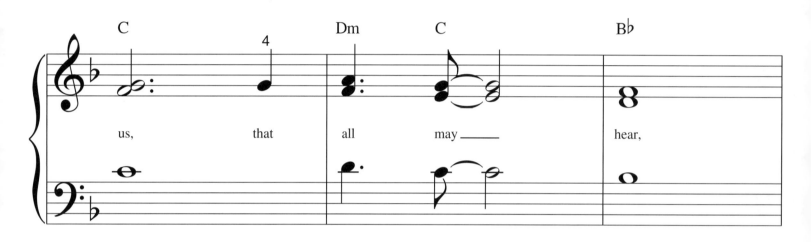
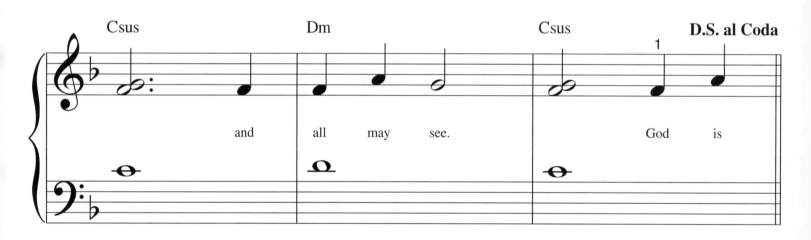
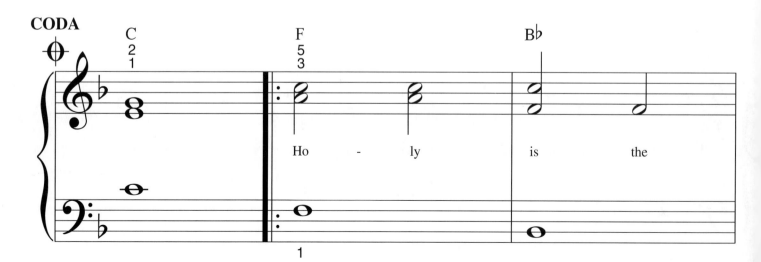

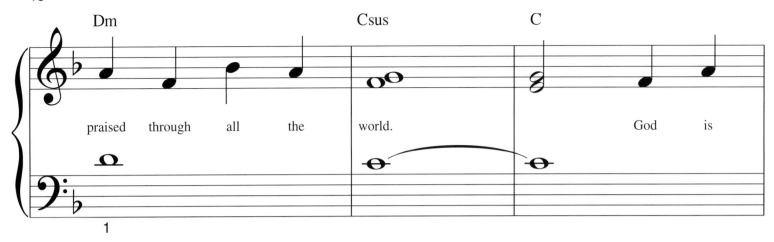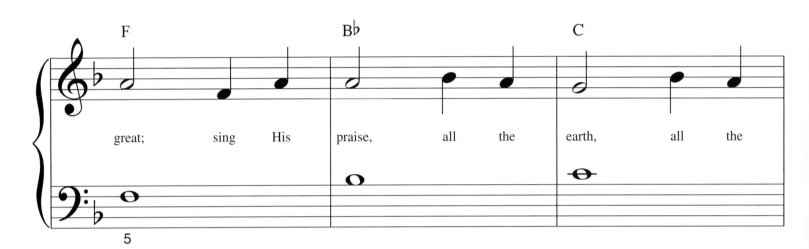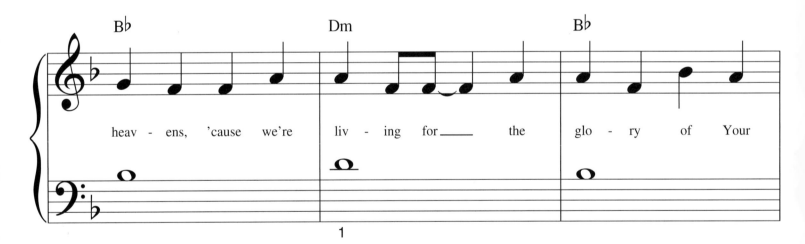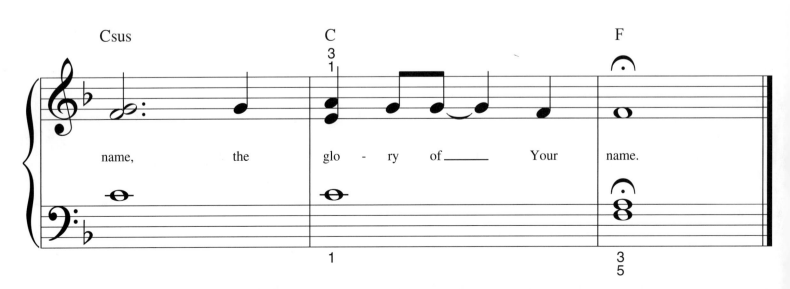

FRIEND OF GOD

Words and Music by MICHAEL GUNGOR
and ISRAEL HOUGHTON

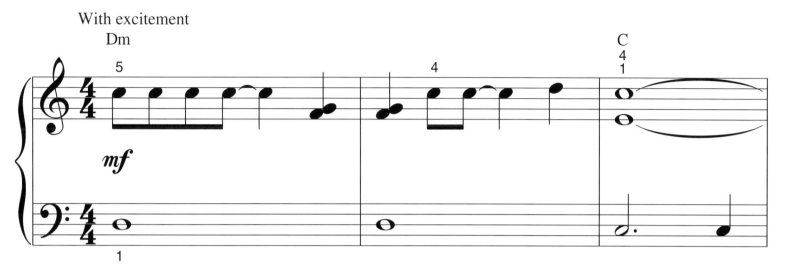

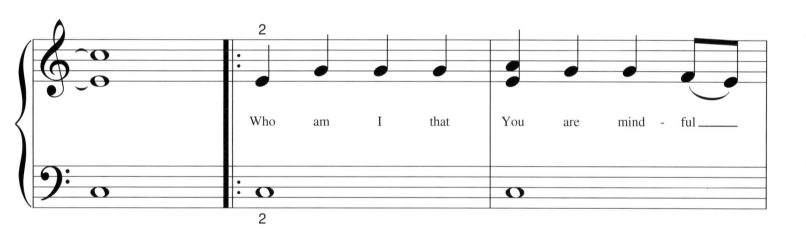

Who am I that You are mind-ful

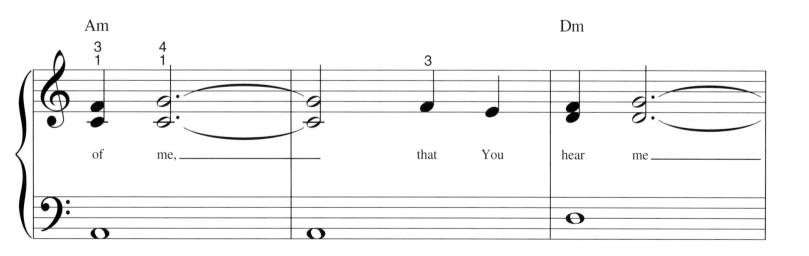

of me, that You hear me

© 2003 Integrity's Praise! Music/BMI and Vertical Worship Songs/ASCAP
c/o Integrity Media, Inc., 1000 Cody Road, Mobile, AL 36695
All Rights Reserved   International Copyright Secured   Used by Permission

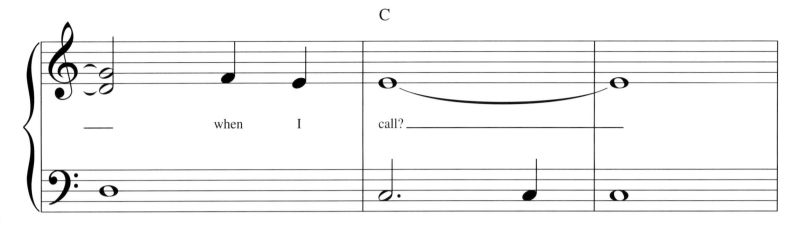
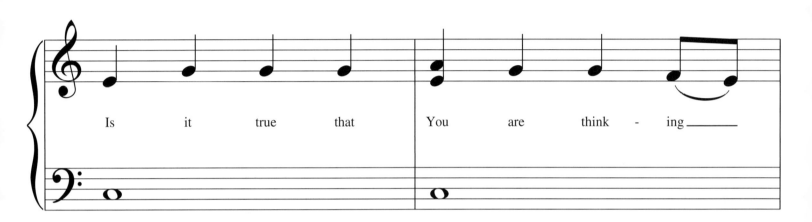
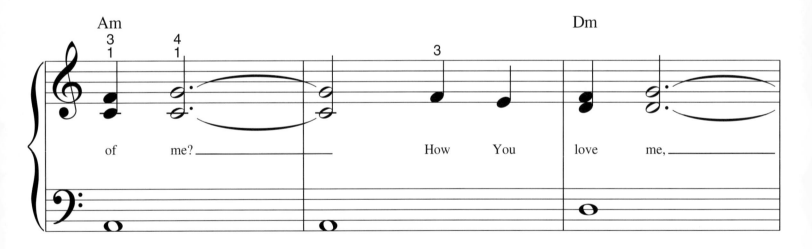
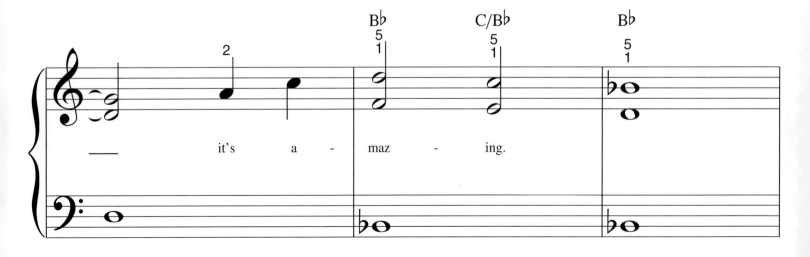

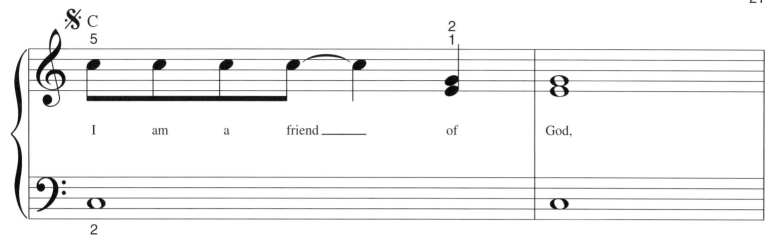

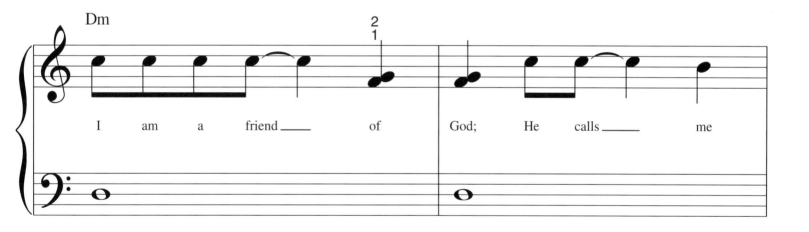
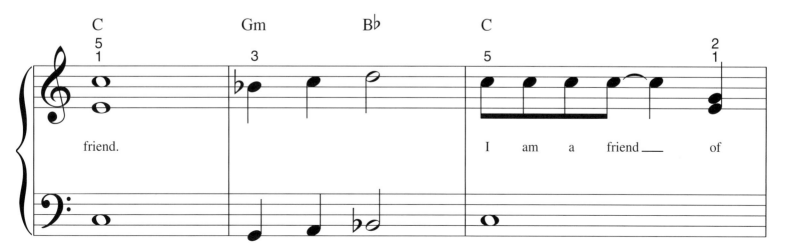

22

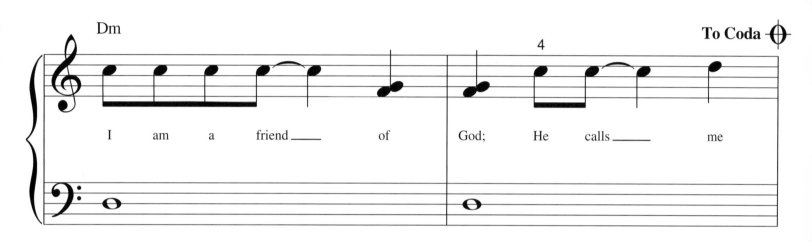

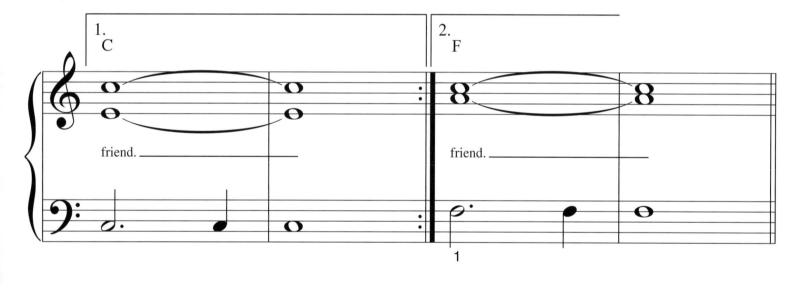

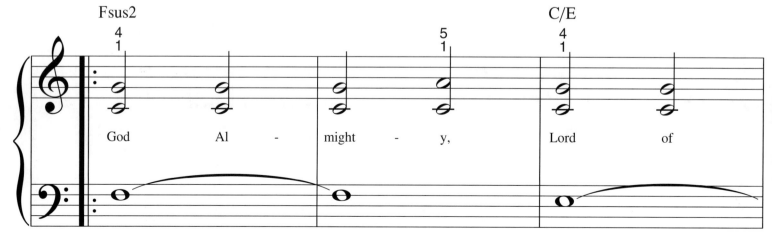

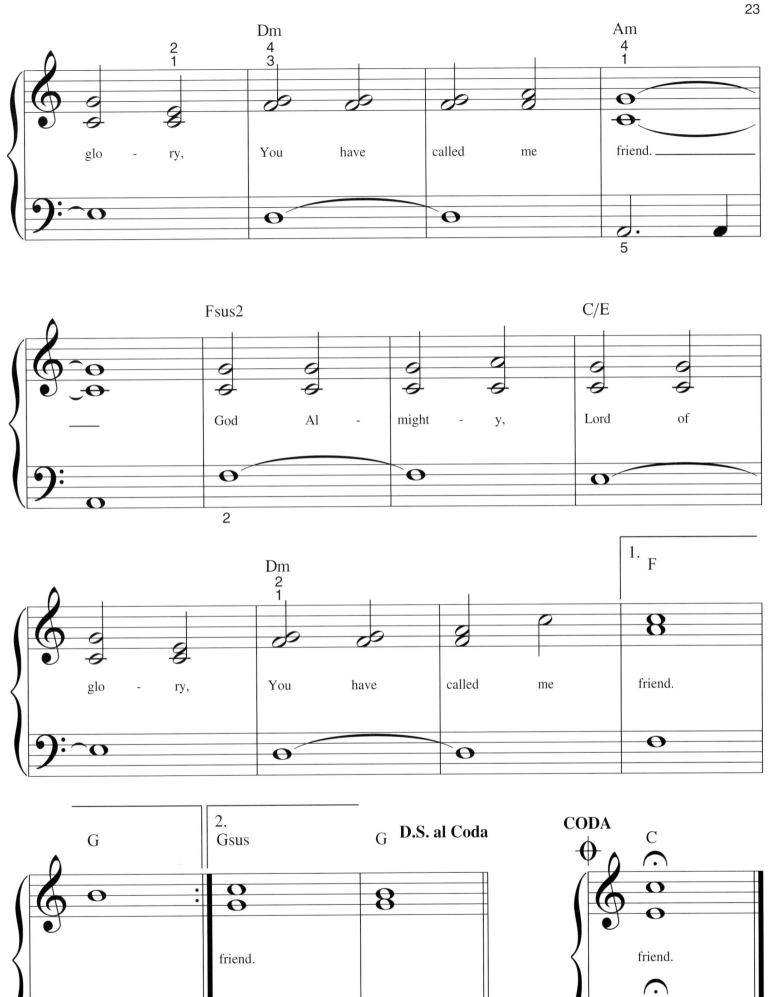

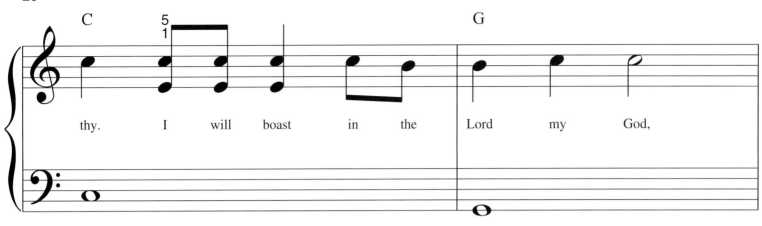
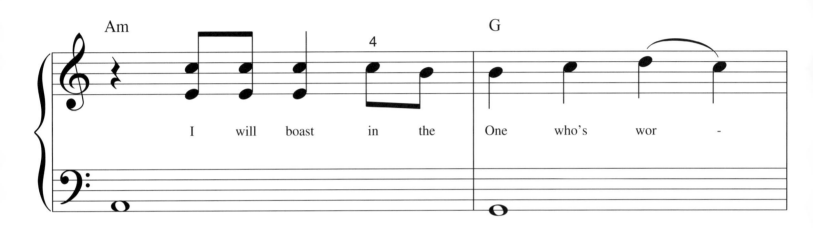

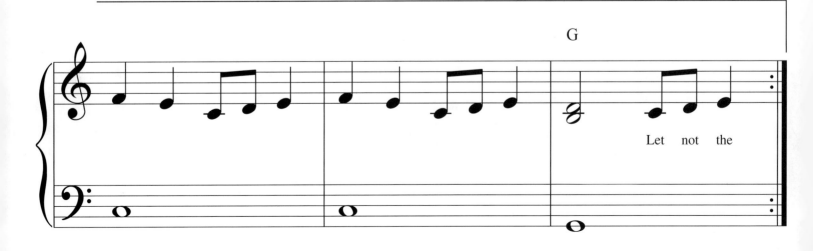

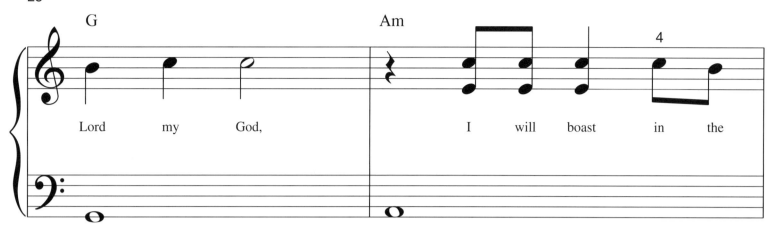
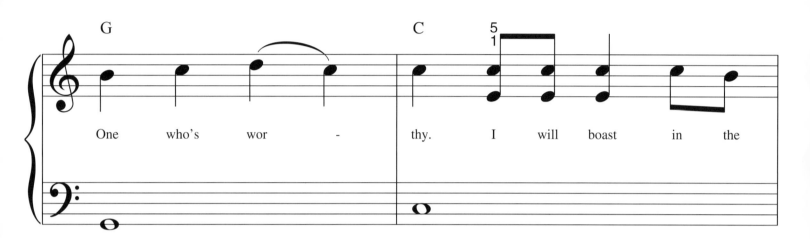
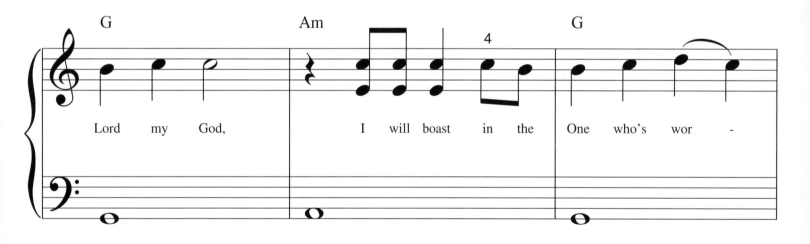

MAJESTIC

Words and Music by
LINCOLN BREWSTER

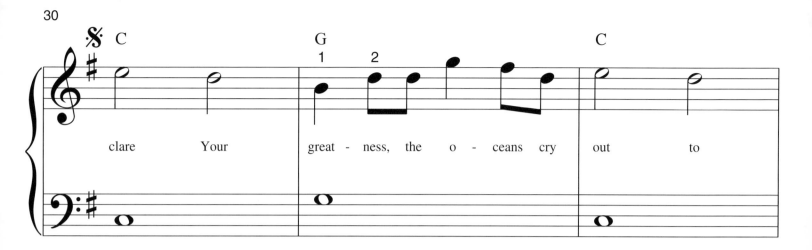
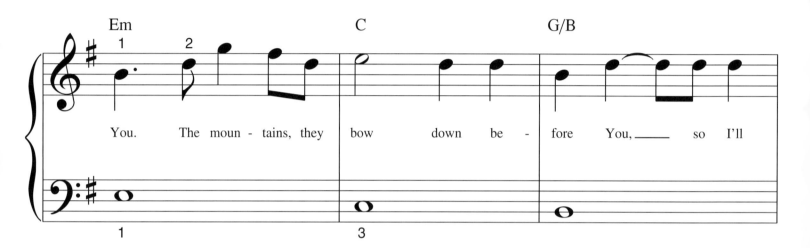
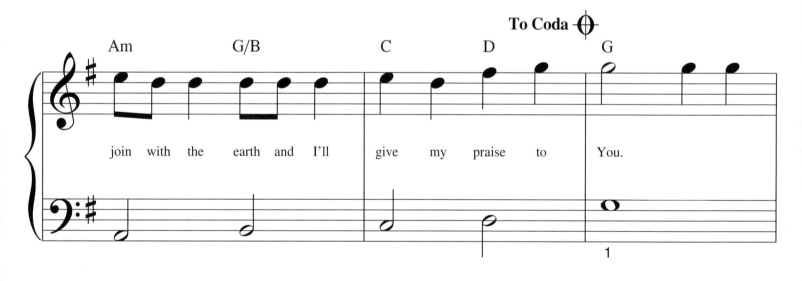
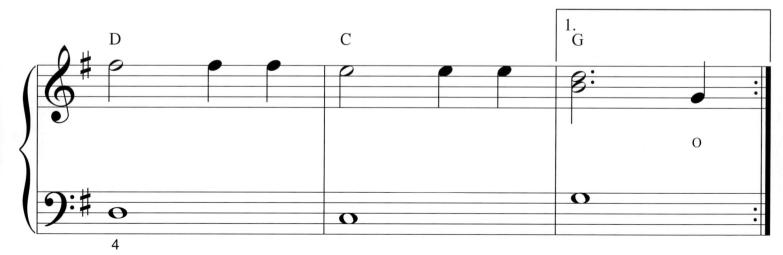

MY BEST FRIEND

Words and Music by JOEL HOUSTON
and MARTY SAMPSON

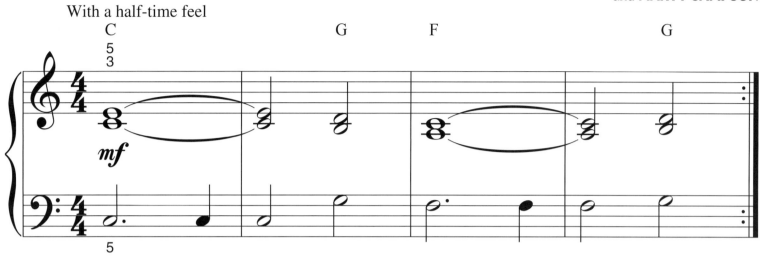
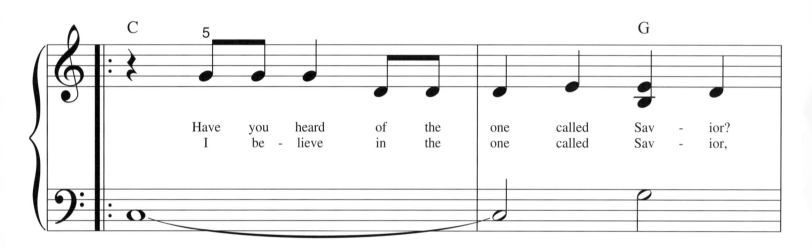
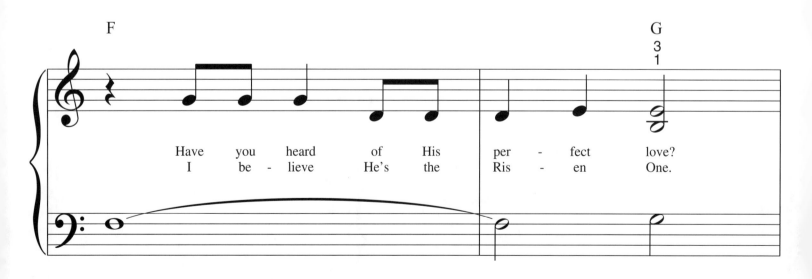

© 2000 Joel Houston, Marty Sampson and Hillsong Publishing (admin. in the U.S. and Canada by Integrity's Hosanna! Music/ASCAP)
c/o Integrity Media, Inc., 1000 Cody Road, Mobile, AL 36695
All Rights Reserved   International Copyright Secured   Used by Permission

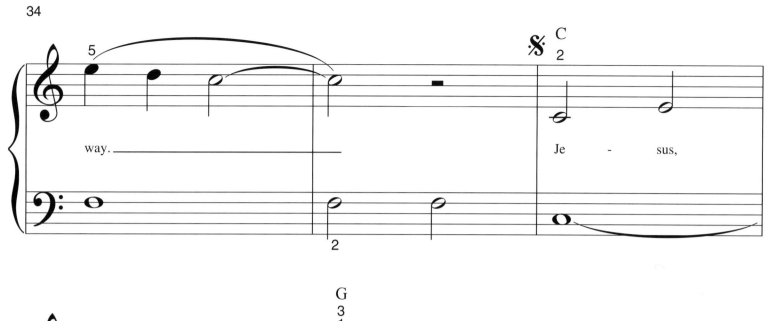
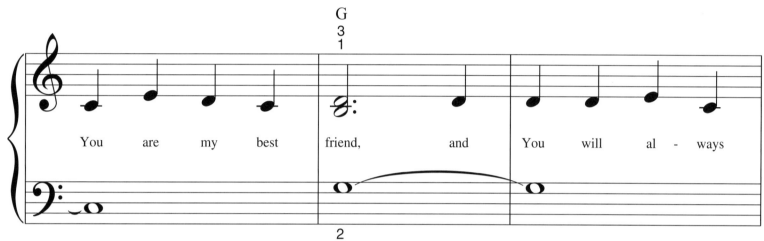
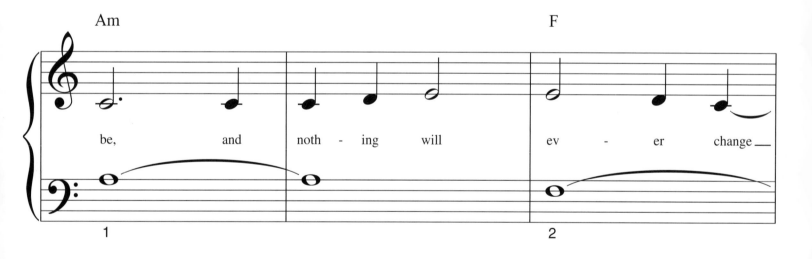
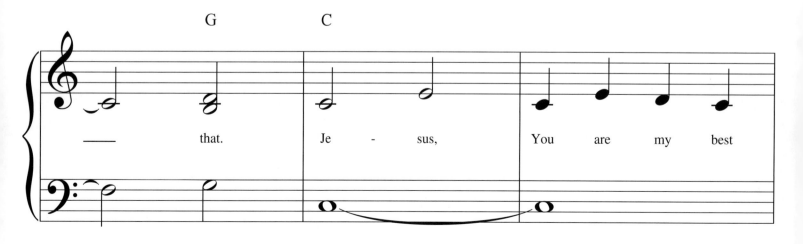

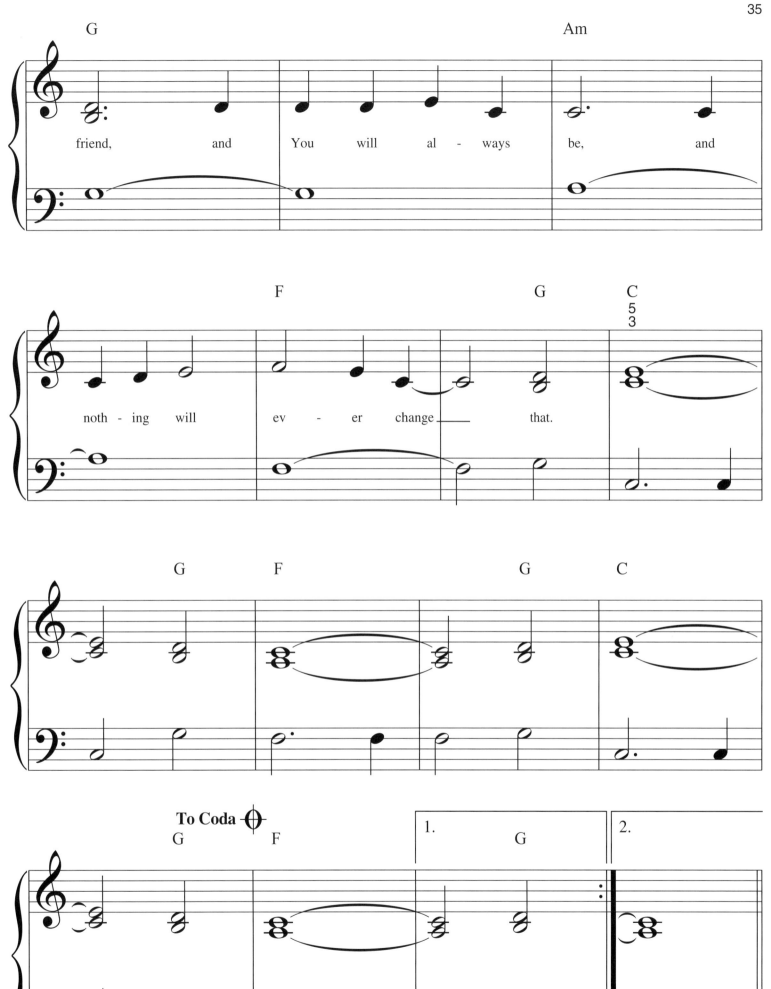

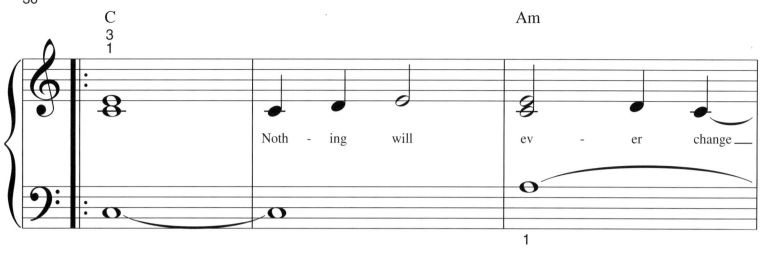
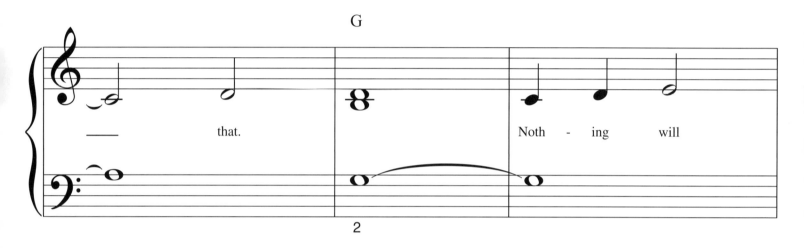

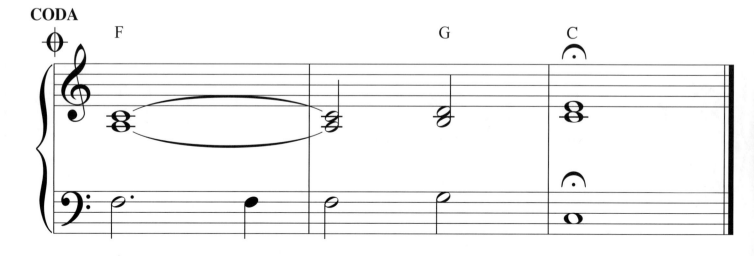

MIGHTY TO SAVE

Words and Music by BEN FIELDING
and REUBEN MORGAN

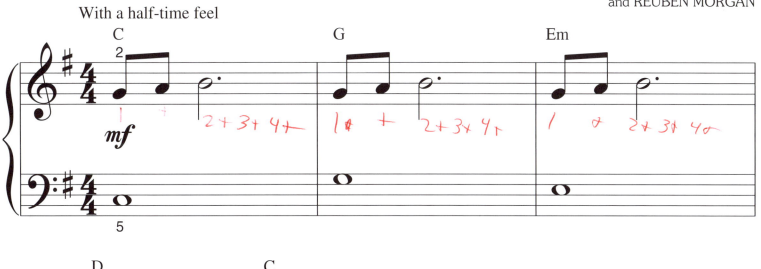
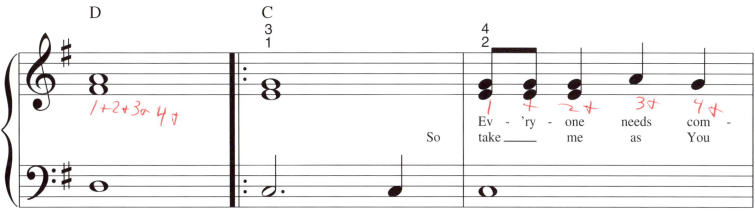
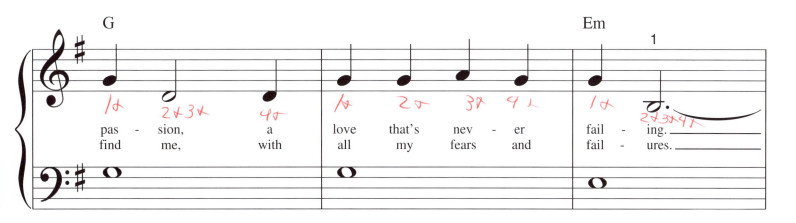
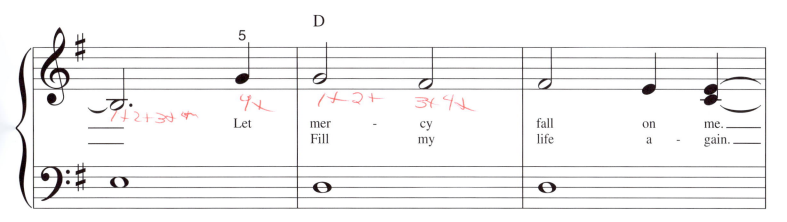

© 2006 Ben Fielding, Reuben Morgan and Hillsong Publishing (admin. in the U.S. and Canada by Integrity's Hosanna! Music)/ASCAP
c/o Integrity Media, Inc., 1000 Cody Road, Mobile, AL 36695
All Rights Reserved   International Copyright Secured   Used by Permission

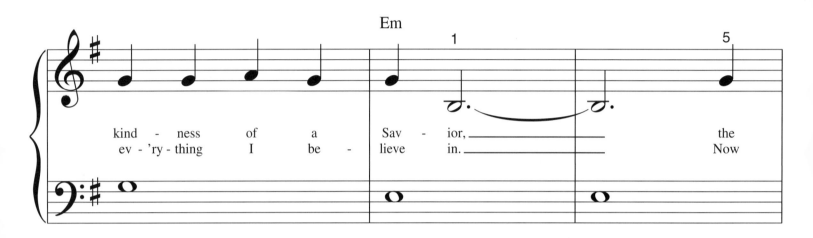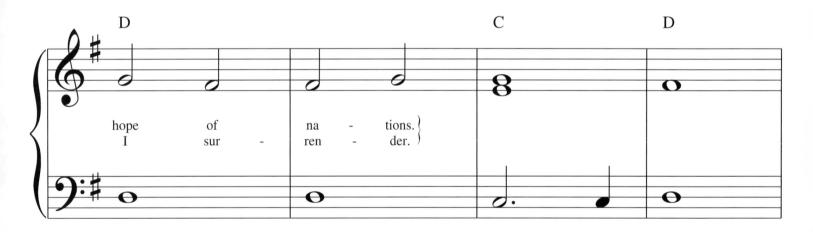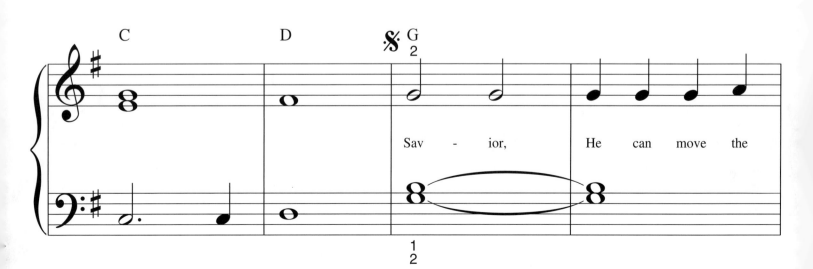

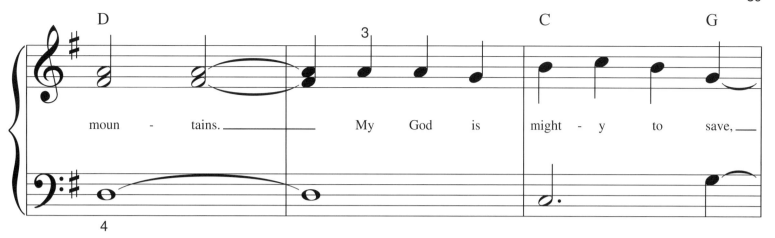
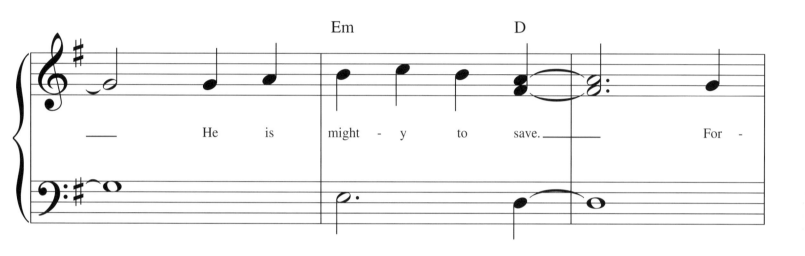
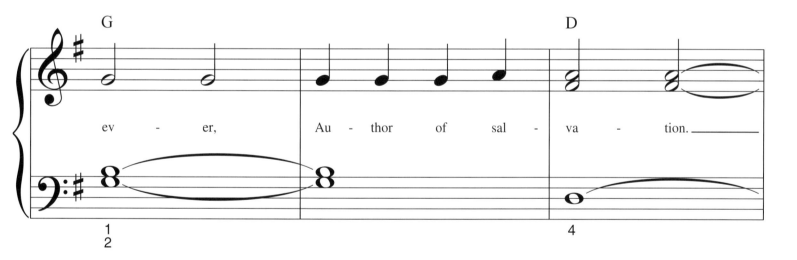
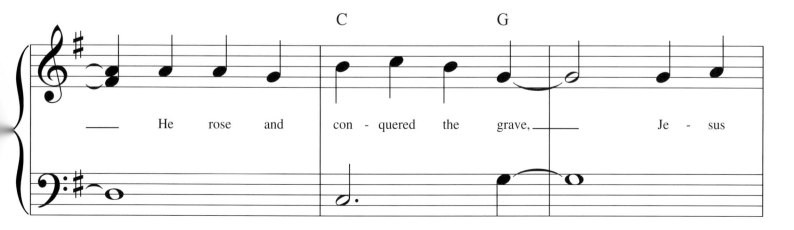

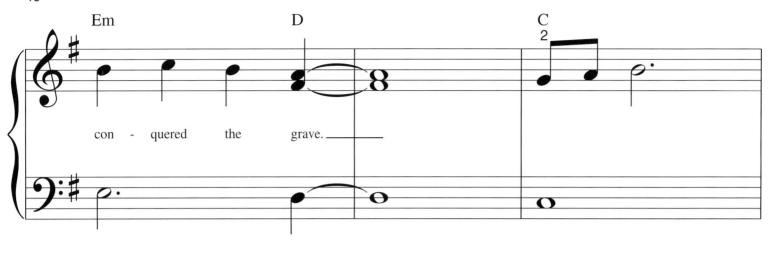
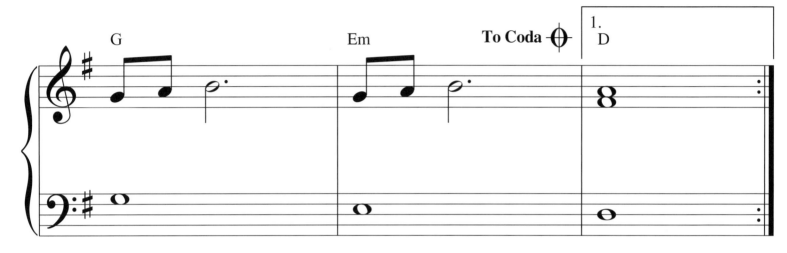
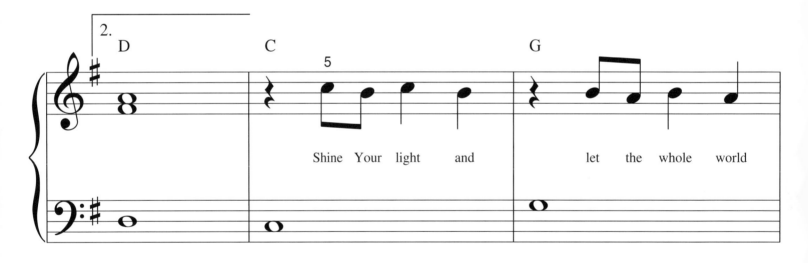

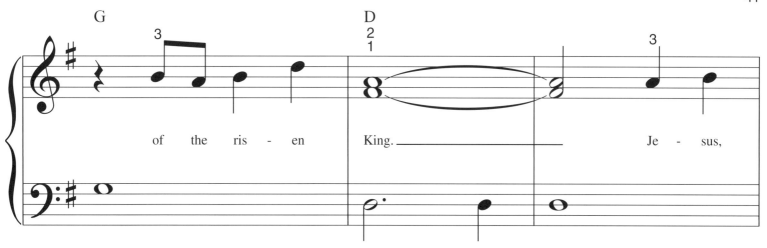

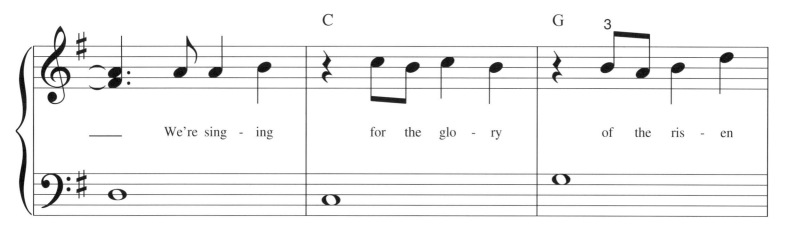
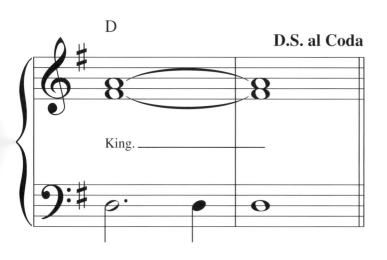
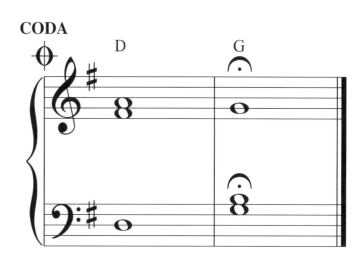

SHOUT TO THE LORD

Words and Music by
DARLENE ZSCHECH

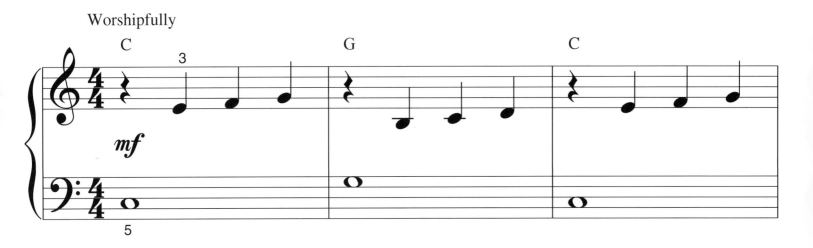
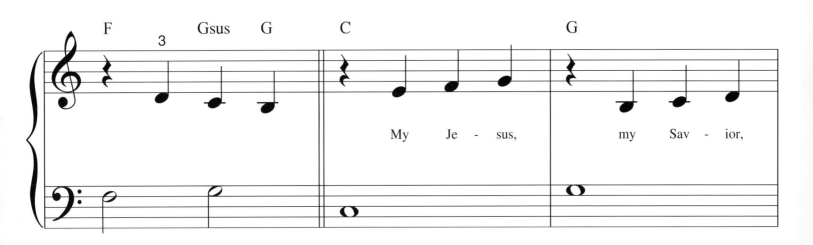
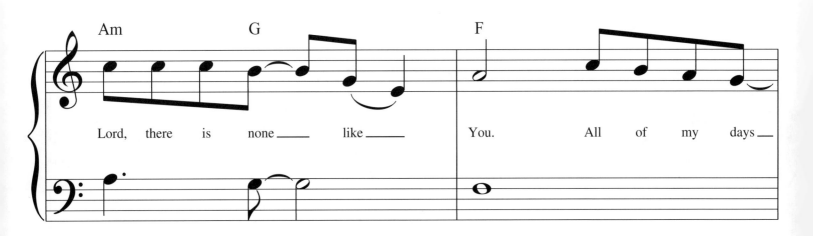

© 1993 Darlene Zschech and Hillsong Publishing (admin. in the U.S. and Canada by Integrity's Hosanna! Music/ASCAP)
c/o Integrity Media, Inc., 1000 Cody Road, Mobile, AL 36695
All Rights Reserved International Copyright Secured Used by Permission

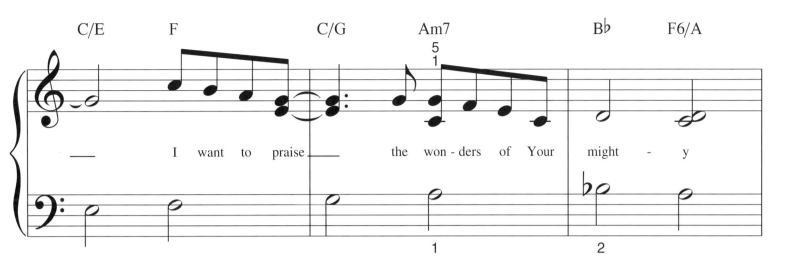
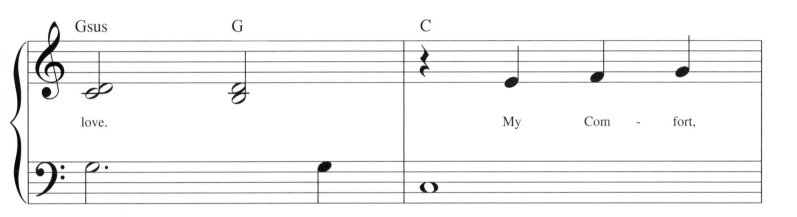
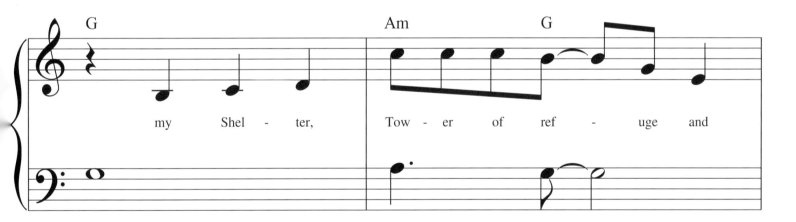
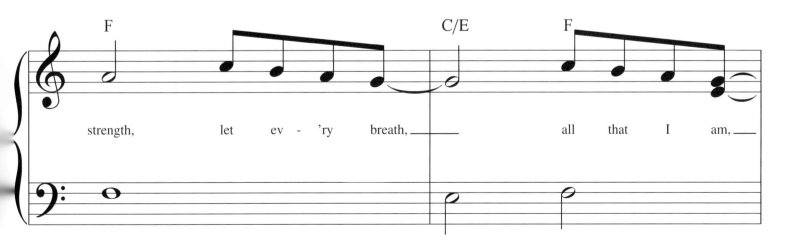

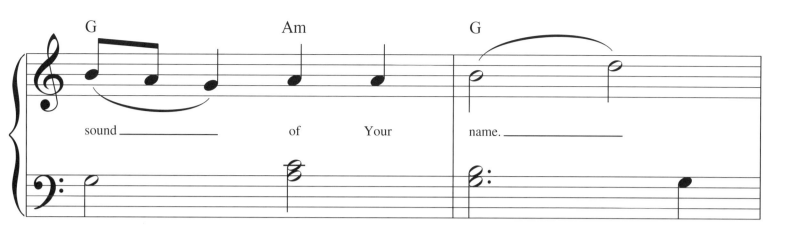
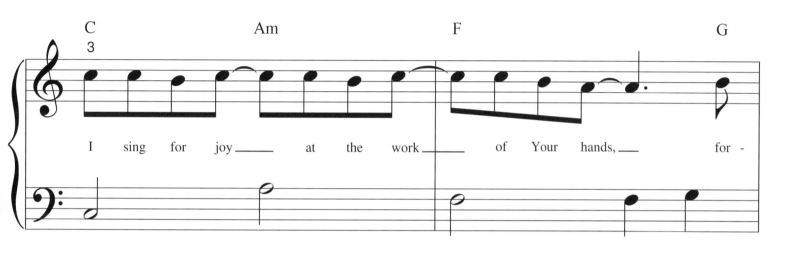

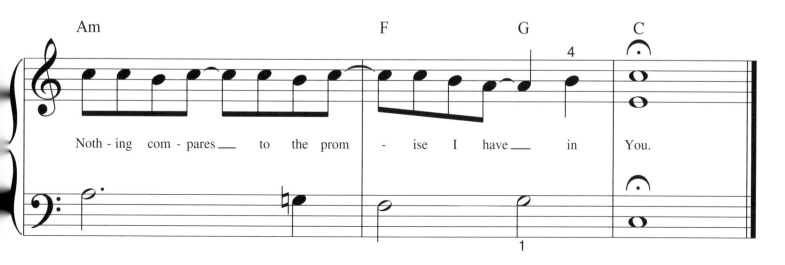

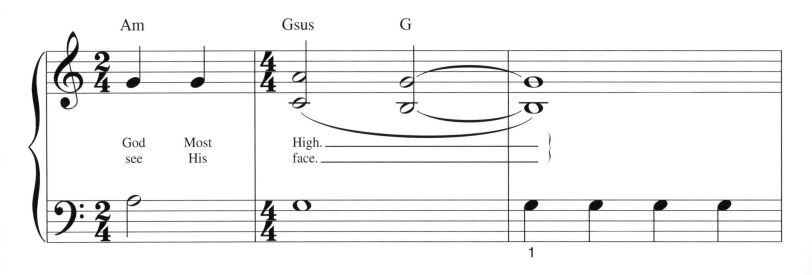
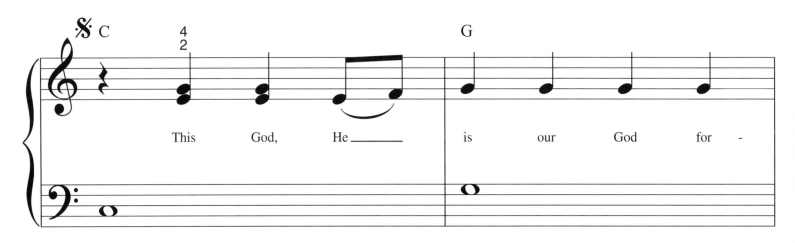
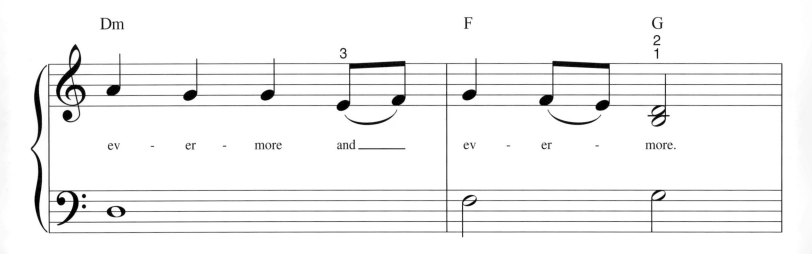

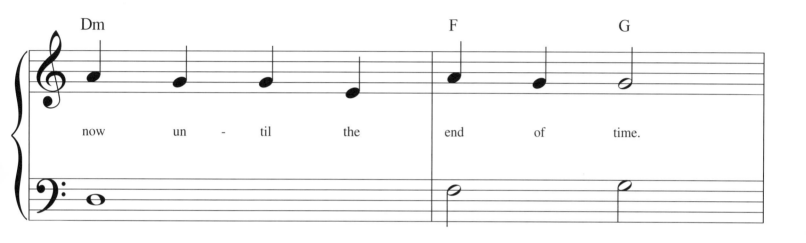
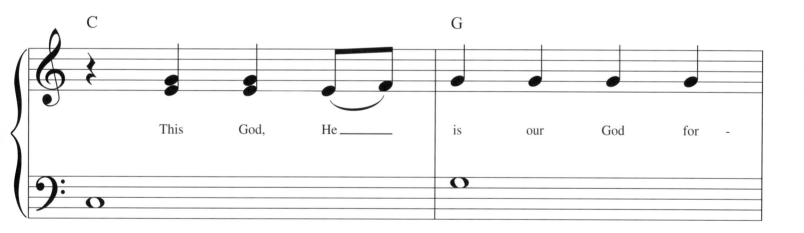
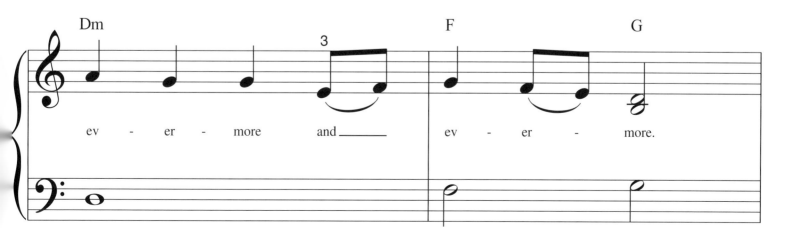

TRUST IN THE LORD

Words and Music by
AMY SANDSTROM-SHROYER

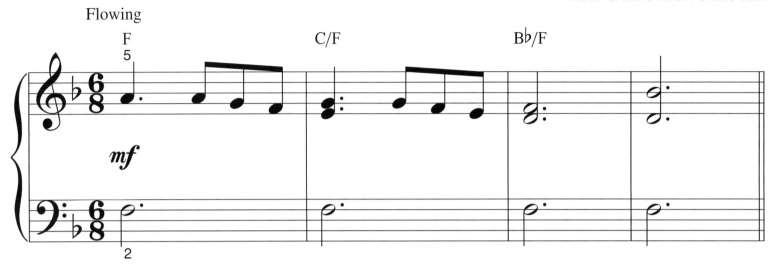
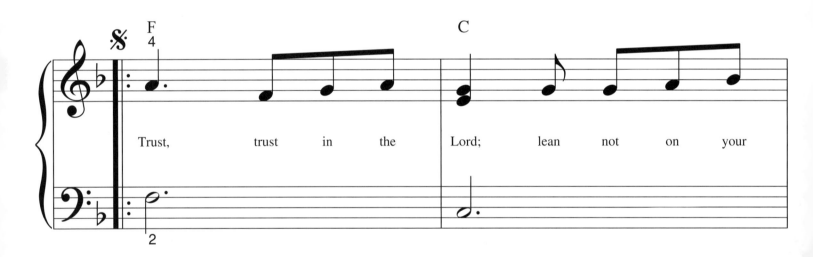
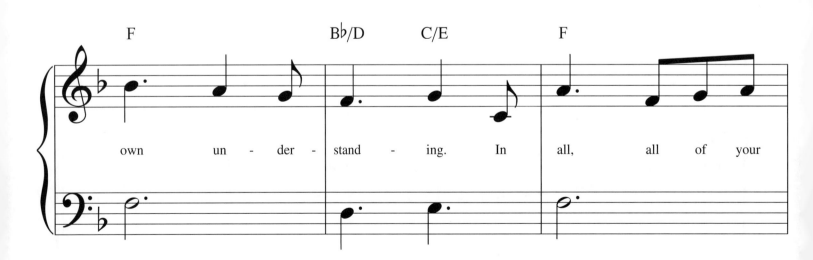

© 1998 Integrity's Hosanna! Music/ASCAP
c/o Integrity Media, Inc., 1000 Cody Road, Mobile, AL 36695
All Rights Reserved   International Copyright Secured   Used by Permission

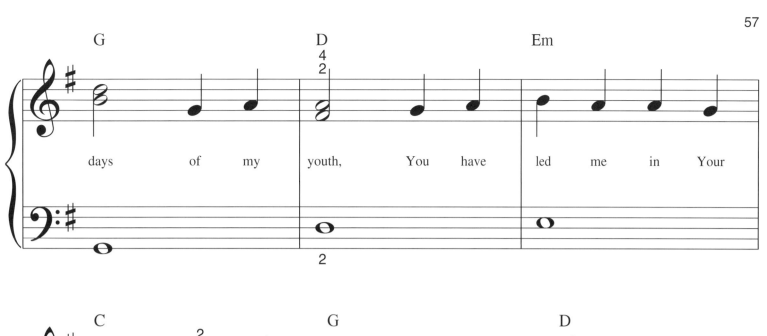
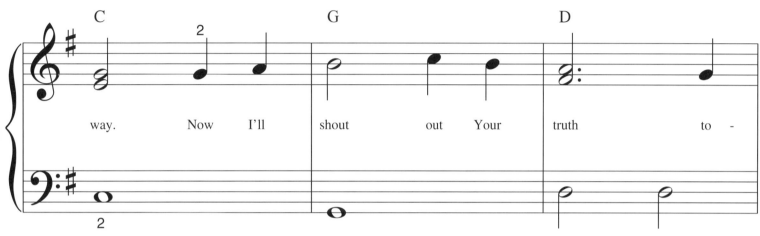
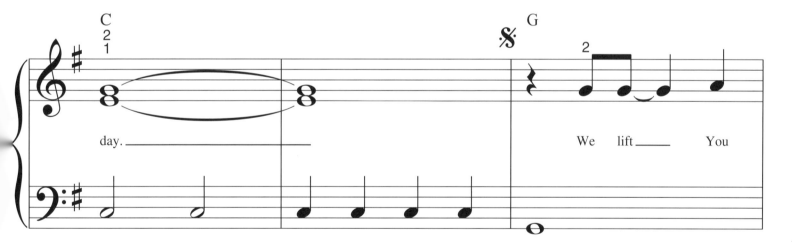

WORSHIP YOU FOREVER

Words and Music by
TODD FIELDS

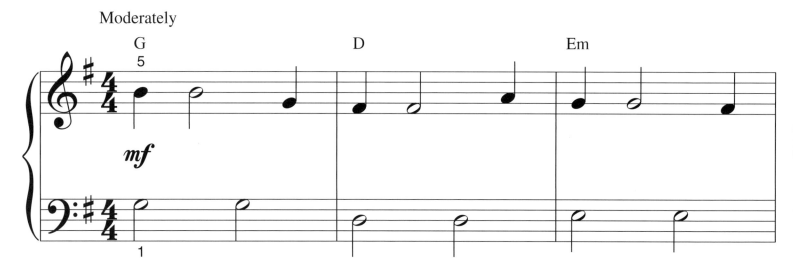
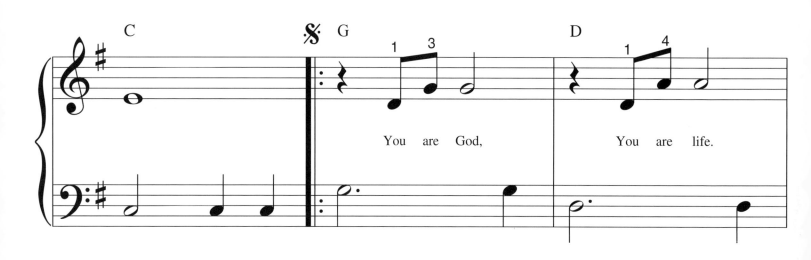
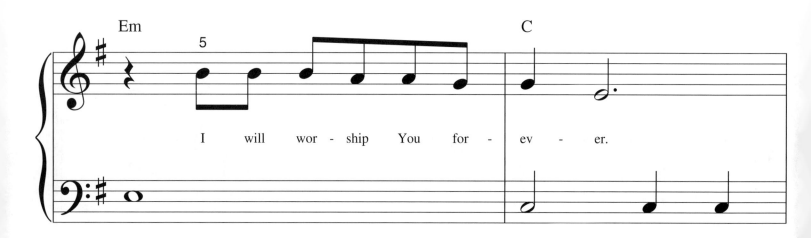

© 2000 Integrity's Praise! Music/BMI c/o Integrity Media, Inc.,
1000 Cody Road, Mobile, AL 36695 and Robinson Lane Music/BMI
All Rights Reserved   International Copyright Secured   Used by Permission

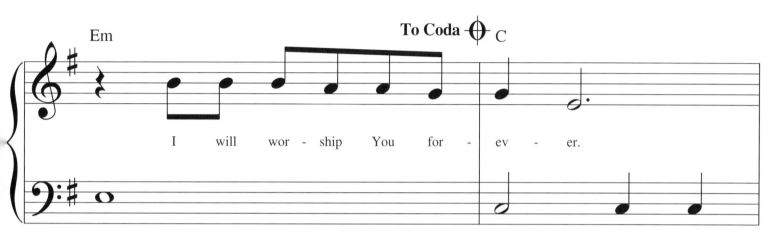
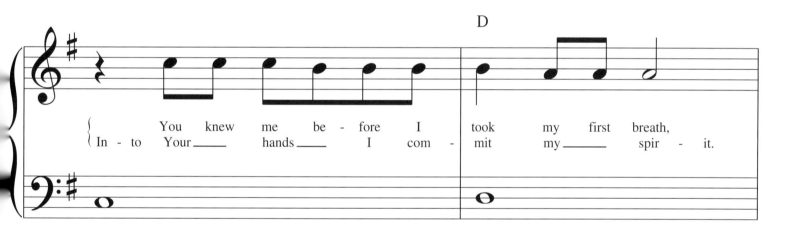
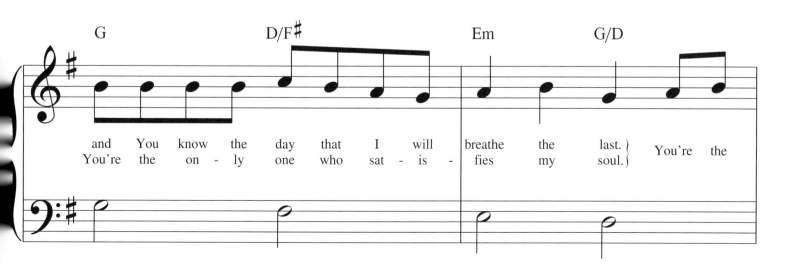

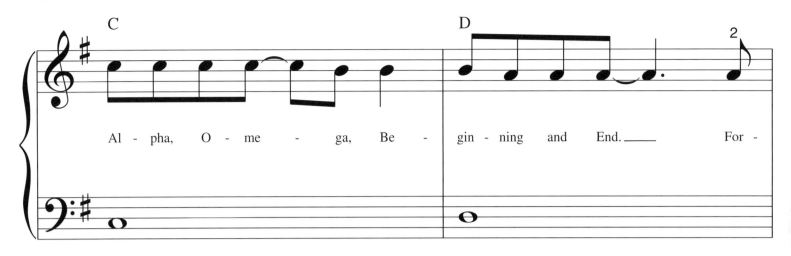
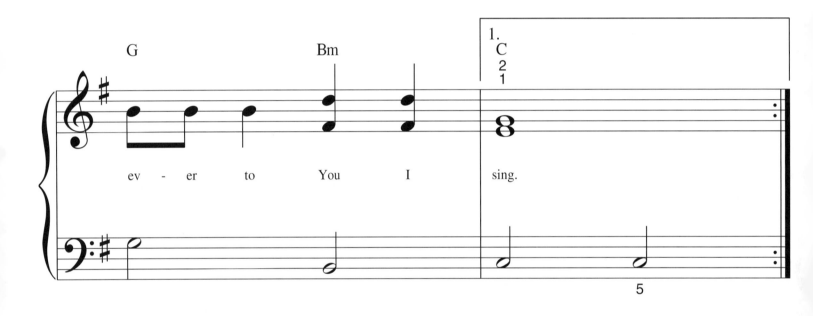

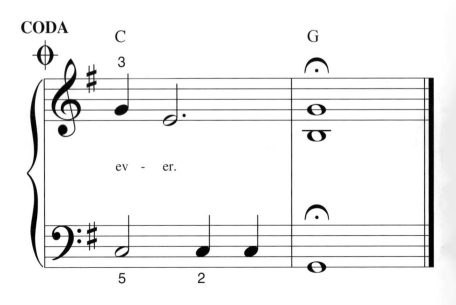

YOU ARE GOOD

Words and Music by
ISRAEL HOUGHTON

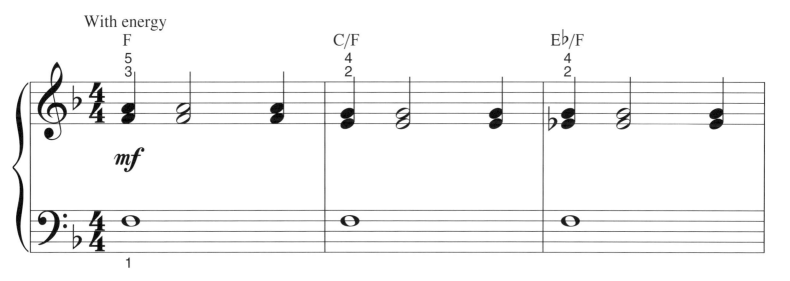

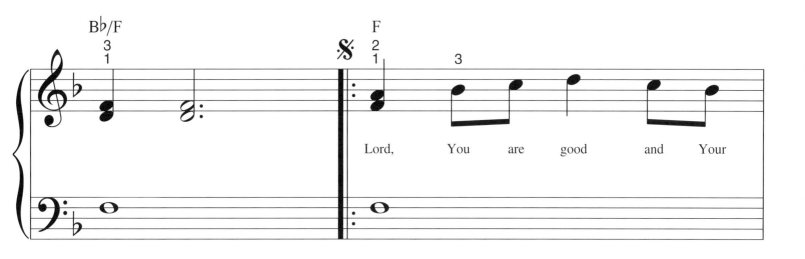

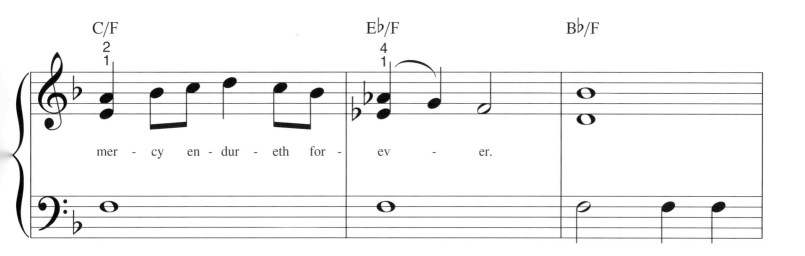

© 2001 Integrity's Praise! Music/BMI
c/o Integrity Media, Inc., 1000 Cody Road, Mobile, AL 36695
All Rights Reserved   International Copyright Secured   Used by Permission

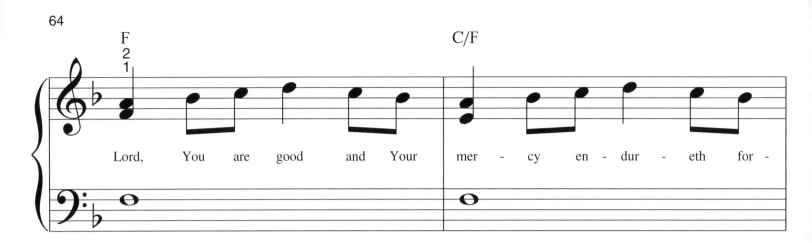
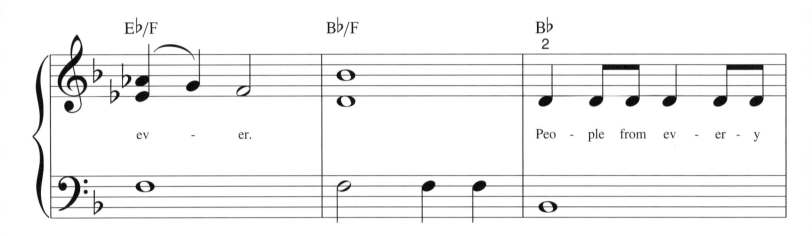
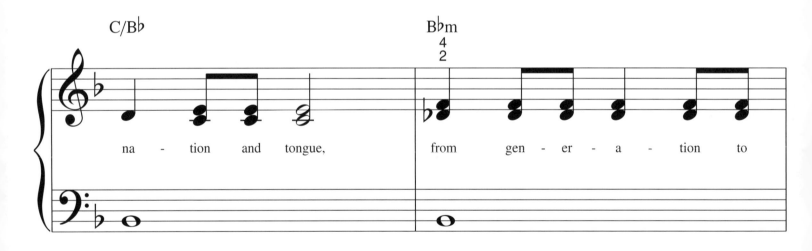
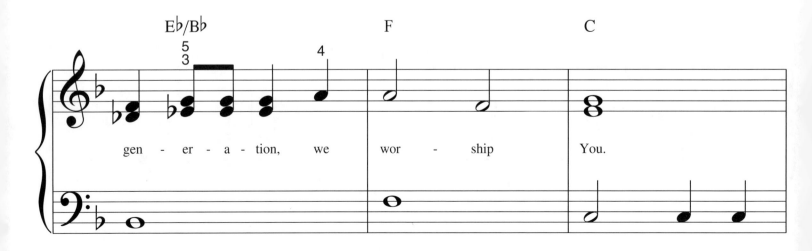

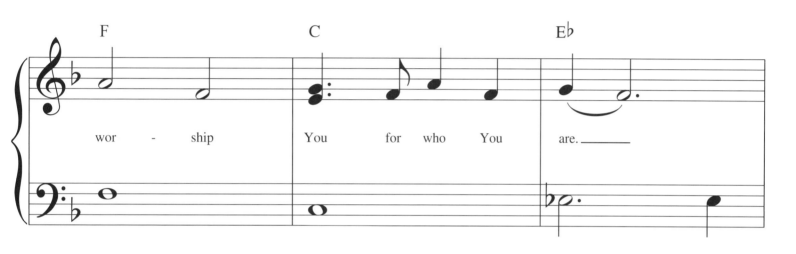
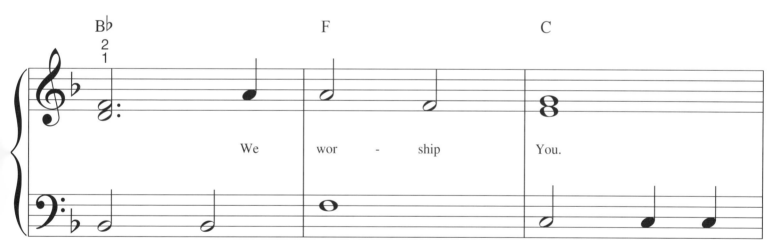
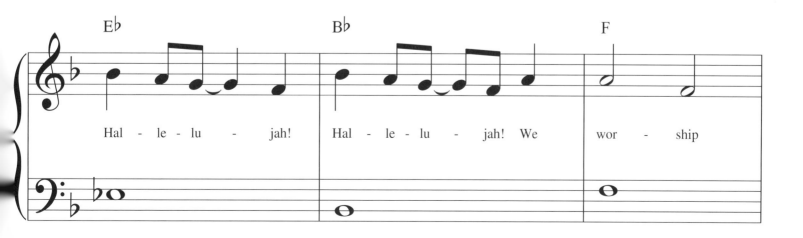

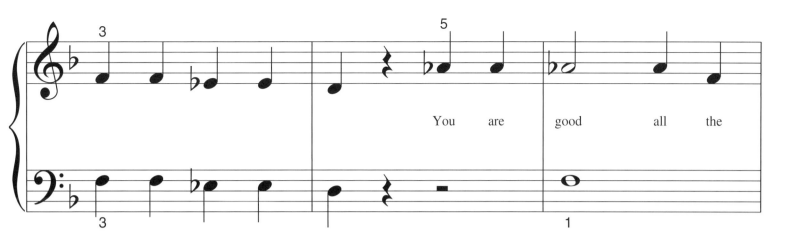

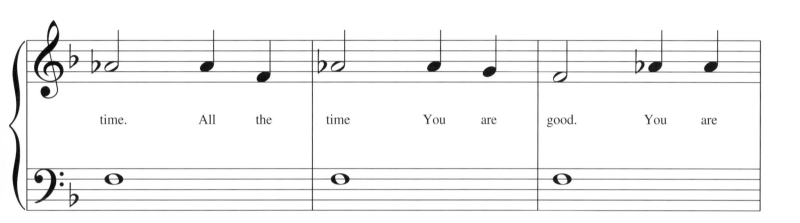

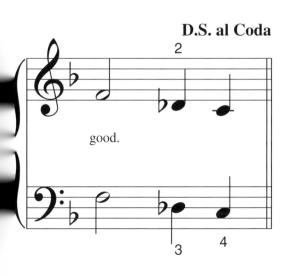

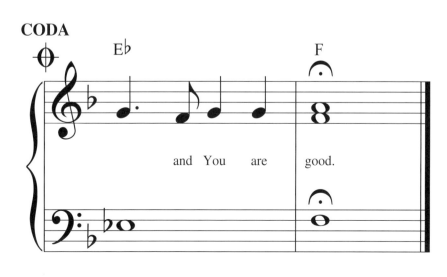

YOUR NAME

Words and Music by PAUL BALOCHE
and GLENN PACKIAM

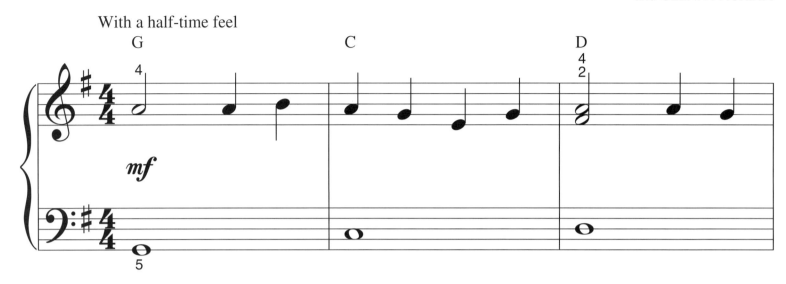
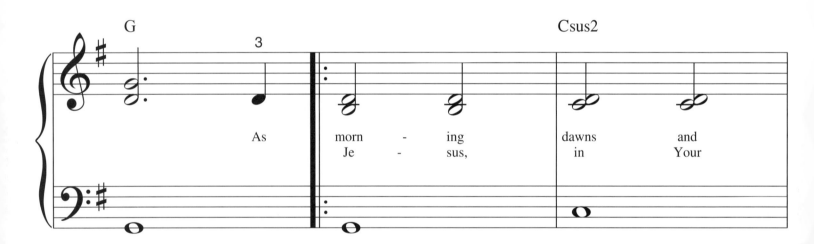
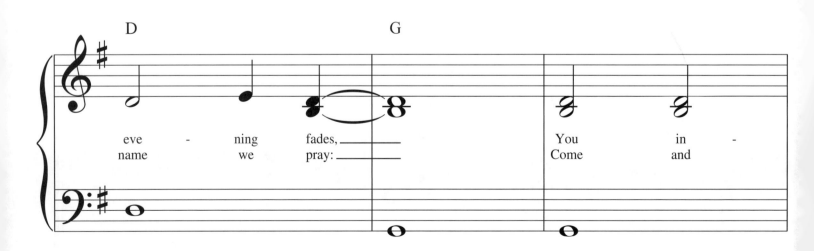

© 2006 Integrity's Hosanna! Music/ASCAP and Vertical Worship Songs/ASCAP
c/o Integrity Media, Inc., 1000 Cody Road, Mobile, AL 36695
All Rights Reserved   International Copyright Secured   Used by Permission

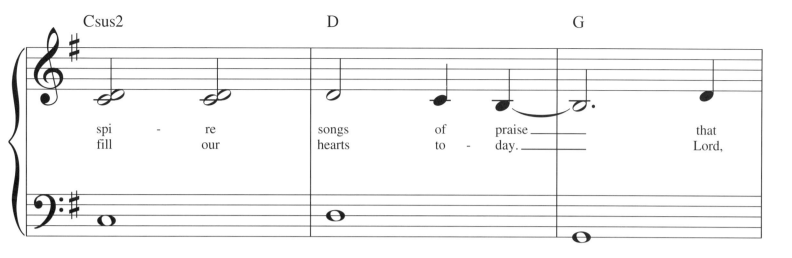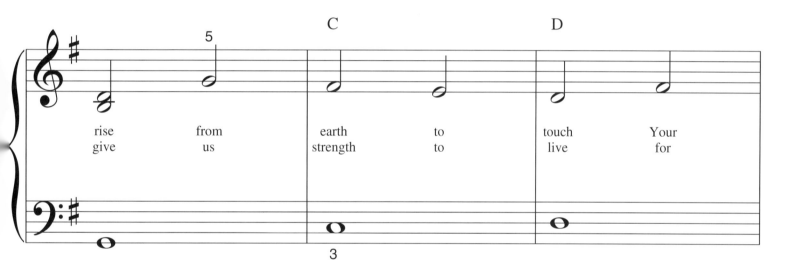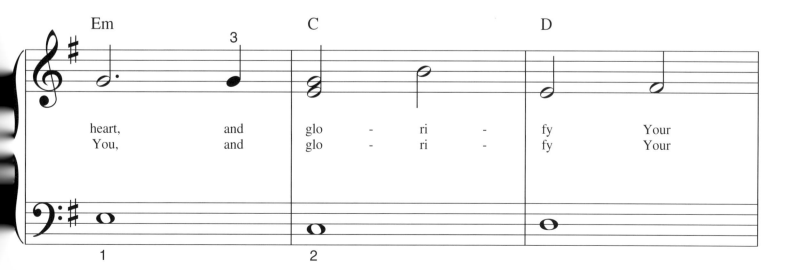

Big Fun With Big-Note Piano Books!
These songbooks feature exciting easy arrangements for beginning piano students.

Beatles' Best
27 classics for beginners to enjoy, including: Can't Buy Me Love • Eleanor Rigby • Hey Jude • Michelle • Here, There and Everywhere • When I'm Sixty-Four • Yesterday • and more.
00222561 ....$10.95

The Best Songs Ever
70 favorites, featuring: Body and Soul • Crazy • Edelweiss • Fly Me to the Moon • Georgia on My Mind • Imagine • The Lady Is a Tramp • Memory • A String of Pearls • Tears in Heaven • Unforgettable • You Are So Beautiful • and more.
00310425 ....$19.95

Children's Favorite Movie Songs
arranged by Phillip Keveren
16 favorites from films, including: The Bare Necessities • Beauty and the Beast • Can You Feel the Love Tonight • Do-Re-Mi • Feed the Birds • The Lonely Goatherd • My Funny Friend and Me • Raiders March • The Rainbow Connection • So Long, Farewell • Tomorrow • Yellow Submarine • You'll Be in My Heart • Zip-A-Dee-Doo-Dah.
00310838 ....$10.95

Classical Music's Greatest Hits
24 beloved classical pieces, including: Air on the G String • Ave Maria • By the Beautiful Blue Danube • Canon in D • Eine Kleine Nachtmusik • Für Elise • Ode to Joy • Romeo and Juliet • Waltz of the Flowers • more.
00310475 ....$9.95

Disney Big-Note Collection
Over 40 Disney favorites, including: Circle of Life • Colors of the Wind • Hakuna Matata • It's a Small World • Under the Sea • A Whole New World • Winnie the Pooh • Zip-A-Dee-Doo-Dah • and more.
00316056 ....$19.95

Essential Classical
22 simplified piano pieces from top composers, including: Ave Maria (Schubert) • Blue Danube Waltz (Strauss) • Für Elise (Beethoven) • Jesu, Joy of Man's Desiring (Bach) • Morning (Grieg) • Pomp and Circumstance (Elgar) • and many more.
00311205 ....$9.95

Elton John – Greatest Hits
16 of his biggest hits, including: Bennie and the Jets • Candle in the Wind • Crocodile Rock • Rocket Man • Sacrifice • Your Song • and more.
00221832 ....$10.95

Favorite Children's Songs
arranged by Bill Boyd
29 easy arrangements of songs to play and sing with children: Peter Cottontail • I Whistle a Happy Tune • It's a Small World • On the Good Ship Lollipop • The Rainbow Connection • and more!
00240251 ....$10.95

The Magic of Disney
13 songs, including: Beauty and the Beast • Can You Feel the Love Tonight • Go the Distance • God Help the Outcasts • A Whole New World • You've Got a Friend in Me • and more.
00310319 ....$10.95

Movie Hits
20 songs popularized on the silver screen, including: Breakaway • I Believe I Can Fly • I Will Remember You • Kokomo • Somewhere Out There • Tears in Heaven • What a Wonderful World • and more.
00221804 ....$10.95

The Phantom of the Opera
9 songs from the Broadway spectacular, including: All I Ask of You • Angel of Music • Masquerade • The Music of the Night • The Phantom of the Opera • The Point of No Return • Prima Donna • Think of Me • Wishing You Were Somehow Here Again.
00110006 ....$12.95

The Sound of Music
arranged by Phillip Keveren
9 favorites: Climb Ev'ry Mountain • Do-Re-Mi • Edelweiss • The Lonely Goatherd • Maria • My Favorite Things • Sixteen Going on Seventeen • So Long, Farewell • The Sound of Music.
00316057 ....$9.95

Today's Pop Hits
14 of today's hottest hits: Beautiful • Clocks • Complicated • Don't Know Why • Drift Away • Fallen • Heaven • A Moment Like This • 100 Years • Pieces of Me • She Will Be Loved • A Thousand Miles • You Don't Know My Name • You Raise Me Up.
00221817 ....$12.95

Worship Favorites
20 powerful songs: Above All • Better Is One Day • Come, Now Is the Time to Worship • Draw Me Close • Forever • Great Is the Lord • The Heart of Worship • I Could Sing of Your Love Forever • More Precious Than Silver • Open the Eyes of My Heart • Shout to the Lord • Worthy Is the Lamb • and more.
00311207 ....$10.95

Prices, contents, and availability subject to change without notice.
Disney characters and artwork © Disney Enterprises, Inc.

Complete song lists online!

For More Information, See Your Local Music Dealer, Or Write To:

HAL•LEONARD® CORPORATION
7777 W. Bluemound Rd. P.O. Box 13819 Milwaukee, WI 53213

www.halleonard.com